POOL PARTIES

JENNIFER MACBAIN-STEPHENS

Table of Contents

POOL PARTIES

Pool Parties I: Donut Rain

Inspired by Yue Li's, "Donut Rain," mixed media installation,
variable size, 2016

A pink inner tube saved us that night
from the reversible swimming pool
that wanted to eat us alive,

stretched over the fake green turf wars
that would become a dentist's editorial smile
so he can say, "look at this image/ It's *so* editorial."

Instead: cling to a fuzzy round body,
not the planets,
hold particle life,
the outside atmosphere too stab happy.

Let me pretend dog paddle,
pretend thigh master,

hide in the closet jumpers,
promote interloper game chaser.

Our fake high society grandeur
is rum and coke empathy

with a touch of blush hedonism.
Do you know what I see

when I look at my reflection?
I don't play the tuba anymore,
so my lip width has diminished,

not enough air
is filling the pipes.

You don't need to hold your breath in
this adult watering hole.

Cotton candy and bronzed busts
always remind me that you

always liked to teach me something.
I saw that in the looking glass tonight,

the mosaic whites and reds of your cheeks
crumbled and you couldn't lift a smile

if it slapped you awake.

Catastrophe swizzle stick,
blame the chocolate,
blame the sea foam,

the plastic walls collapse darling.
Blow down this marshmallow
flush house, / cauterize the front door wound.

I was always a grey hound skitter kind of girl.

Onward Gemini

For H.

Daughter is a light puffy jacket,
contains a forest inside,

she flops, she tosses schoolery
a different kind of note,

redecorates with candles,
laughs at 5 second videos.

Daughter scamps and skates,
she daisy dukes,

loses green Viking volleyball shorts,
 flattens warm pita,

filters the like show,
 size ten shoe already.

Giraffe daughter teeters
between flat and heel,

ponytail and bun,
brown eyed Clearasil,

holds a candle for cartoons,
maybe a too long hug devastates the world,

opinions fall off the roof,
no earth below her feet.

_____: rooms I would build

to see the vulnerable me
to honor short haired dogs who are gone
hi fy to tune minimum wage out
lo fy to turn nostalgia on
to get slippery with a body
to ignore mess
to give real compliments
to breathe five breaths in downward dog
to wipe off muddy boots from a garden that burned
to Red Bull refresh
to code magic
to say I love you
to try on Prada
to play disc golf
to roast middle school field trips
to draw future brain maps
to jump around to House of Pain
to fight like we mean it
to build on additional rooms
to deal with compartmentalization issues

to not overschedule

to not color code

to not nap so much

to not shower so little

to not stare at the wall

to not wonder what to do next

to not put on a dress just for Zoom

to not wonder about the future

to not cry

to not feel despair

to not not touch you

to not miss you

to not think about death

to not feel so alone in a room

Tubes

She lays in the hospital bed, a tube in her chest, her blond hair not the usual shine, her glasses on the side table, she cannot laugh or cry at her mother's death three days ago or the tube inserted in her chest will become displaced and it's draining fluid. I show up to show my love, moments like this one and that one are already gone, and the next minute hasn't happened yet, and we say, *yeah, yeah maybe,* and, *could you,* and try to speak and breathe but not laugh, don't you dare laugh, because life is serious and precious and if you laugh you might die. I'm the one who told you about that article I read about Lord Yama walking the earth, looking to take the sick away with him to the underworld, and the cold weather, the dark winter days, the death of a mother, and she cannot cry, cannot laugh, sucks air down a tube.

Using an Inclinometer to Design a Mountain Bike Trail in the Woods

The inclinometer is tied to him,
literally hangs around his neck,

we walk up and down in the woods,
the sun gets lower and lower

behind the trees,
he raises it to his eye.

It's hard to keep steady
while measuring the grade of the earth,

cold feet and fingers
while making a bike trail

in West Des Moines, Iowa
crossing frozen creeks,

the tree branches start to look like
upside down spiders in the sky,

webs spiking into gray clouds,
stars brighter away from the city.

We march up and down,
talk about how fast a cyclist will

descend or
climb.

The inclinometer wavers,
trembles,

as we look through it,
line it up with our mouth or nose

to see how the ground rises and falls,
.5 here or a -8 there.

Our faces blend with the lines and dots till new faces are
          made,
always malleable, memories in the woods.

The Play Starts Late

The play starts late, and I'm still trying to save Tasmanian
     devils from themselves.

I drown in plastic bags, and we always knew they were such
     murderers.

One character wears reused cotton but a member of the 1%
     waits in the wings, all white beard like a tiny god,

dreams of producing nano plastics. His vanity plate says
     "bcawzIcn."

One character asks, *where have all of the birds gone?*

A month of record rain and giant squirrels have eaten all
     roots away.

The dirt does not stay in the ground.

Brad Pitt builds one more house for a family dressed in tie
dye.

A neon green snow mobile wreaks Colorado.

A slaughtered calf is red and white like Madonna's skin.

How many working poor groan into their day, the
prologue.

A friend once asked: why give secrets away in the prologue?
Why hold details back from the book?

Greenland's first line: how cold is this polar vortex?

The Director's attention glued to a GoPro of awesome.

The ice sheets in this theater are melting and this makes the
audience cry.

Everyone checks their phones.

If this theater melted at once that would raise sea levels all at
once 7 meters,

people's pearls float away,
the show posters float for rats.

You Were Raised by Bears

You couldn't stand the smothering nature of your mother who you cannot visit now. You like petite girls and she is all hair and girth and tossing you about. She might find some berries for you to eat but not give you enough freedom during coronavirus quarantine. The males are supposed to be competitive in the spring and violent. Where do you rate? Tourists pay $10,000 to watch bears lumber around Alaska with a tour guide. The people dress in khakis and bring tiny fold out chairs solely for this activity of watching bears. The only protection they have against your mother charging at them is bear spray and their own instinct for when something is about to go down, and that maybe they shouldn't sit so close together. They wear masks. You want to go with these khaki wearing people when they sleep on their yacht at night and drink, but you can't. You can only leave the cave now to forage for food. You cannot romp with other bears. Your life was already pretty solitary. Now it is a gray cloud. You also cannot smoke pot or play video games and the cave is cold and you fight with other bears who come too close to you. One day, you will probably lose your temper and go out to play with other bears and maybe get into trouble and a bear might maul you out of frustration. Then you can never get to see Okkervil River in concert, in Portland, every again.

Freeloader

The barnacle is socially challenged; it is a virus cell invasion.

The barnacle takes too long at the snack stand.

The barnacle is a solid paper doll. It stands idle, watches
      you when you think you're alone.

The barnacle pays child support.

The barnacle is not a fast-food nation, but it understands
      the needs of many.

The barnacle is scientifically unnamed at this Bristol
      conference,
but the barnacle is telepathic, so it's a work breakfast.

The barnacle is a scientist's nightmare:
it grows tentacles from the lab's largest pie graph,

beckons the FED to pose for TIME's magazine's cover:
rage is all you need to take that first step toward mob
                mentality.

The barnacle takes a swig of whiskey,

opens

the earth.

Monitor, Monitor

The shift key, a trickster,
the em dash, a tea drinker.

The ENTER square, too open all night.

Keys f5 and f6: obtuse, but
the backspace: loyal.

The plus/minus twins grade school bullies.
The colon a dirty joke,

the page ups and downs, so 1995,

the exclamation point: such a broet, the count-down to my
low battery life.

Warnings blink from green,
to yellow, to *Go Home*

and get your power cord. While you are there,

grab a coupon for Travelocity, a spark of life.

Pool Parties II: If You Had Thrown Me That Life Preserver or Beverage Cart

I didn't know how to shake myself out
of playing with this brass band,

of dissolving small and out of
my goddamn mind.

An over under fraction is equal to
a difference in gorgeousness,

play it both ways,
rub and burn.

Cramp up,
say *Stop*. Offer a mild

shock if you want it,
my correspondent

studied strange beasts,
I took it from her:

the details on automatic
pilot,

a Dixie beer,
a pickup,

my breath like chicory
stripped between windows,

finger the ice and let's go,
a dead Czech actor is

like a funeral:
terrible and beautiful.

I don't want to stop,
can't stop.

This is a found poem. Text from Rice, Anne. *Exit to Eden*.
New York: Harper Collins, 1985. Print. Pages 208–217.

Flint (SiO₂)

She said, how do I find space in the gray and blue sky,
the red gneiss and schist layers?
Step off the ledge.

Flint: often ignored as plain and unappealing,
the beauty of an object is not only in its appearance
but in its potential uses.

Humans are made of dust, but their hearts are the color of
        pink feldspar.
No guard rails surround the towering Kissing Couple.
Grand Junction High School cannot pay for doors on the
boys' bathroom stalls.

A girl with oval glasses tells a trans person that the weather
        is bipolar,
"I've already been soaked and sunned."
A roasted house of loud dams and triple passes.

The surfaces become powdery-white
on exposure to air needs careful storage.

I catch a view all copy products in the high desert,
meanwhile the barista is leggings and hips,
says this is the best kind of subduction

used for making fire and

coffee while Tupac plays on the high-altitude speaker,
and the rain,
and the rain,
and the rain
messes
with our bones, our tectonic plates.

Note: the words in italics in these poems are taken from
Essential Guide to Crystals by Simon and Sue Lilly, 2006,
2010, and 2018. published by Watkins Media Limited.
United Kingdom.

Dubuque, Iowa: Winter

ravaged by unloving,

a pungent likeness is a surge of feeling but also a similarity,
the camper driven back

after flood waters receded,
a picture on her phone: her body in water,

a gesture, a hand wave behind us,
the river crashes goodbye,

a flow chart,
the precip fast and cold,

he says, *should I pick her up?*
to avoid the ice storm

people help one another
when mailboxes freeze shut,

the moisture that disappears from lips into air,

he sits near
chipped off ice from the truck,

the curls around his forehead
exaggerated in the snow,

he repeats words like *giant,*

our depleted strength,
the way a chest rises and falls into meadows

then flips over,

how we spread our arms in bed,
who is this new bird that cries above me

in the grayness everywhere?

Solstice

beard crush,
smash open teeth,

I'd pay for your lip
service but

never knew it
felt like a car crash,

to be sore in
new places,

hip rug burns,
sing sonnet-like

about his forearms,
his third thumb removal

scar, every new touch
starting over,

you never barked *stay,*
I flew crow-like,

still chained to trees,
your leaves burned red

and ignition blue,
glass eyes,

syllables, and coffee grounds
scattered the sink's edge,

you never wanted to scan
my brain map,

I let the wasps fly
into the house,

looking to guide
a sweet sting out of my cellar skin.

Crocodile Eyes

half closed,
one bird in the mouth

is worth two dead
floating in salt water.

Let brown eyes beckon a chickadee
fly over fireplace stone,

polished granite in a
warm bath, turn gray eyes green

or sand color: an Amish made table
twice prayed over,

some eyes dip: drugged and red
spread over a sick tiger's eye in meditation.

I never knew how blue
could bite and twist,

slice my cheek
and throat in one blink,

freeze my blush
before it spread.

I would've stayed in
your ice forever

if you let me. Your turquoise
ocean aloof set to swell at the wrong

moon times, my
passion cycle falling

off next month's calendar,
dread pumped sleeping hours

into my chest
too many times,

my green eyes pried open
by tiny game pencils,

tears falling,
each dawn the

orbs raw.
Like a cyclops I fumble

through my carpet cave,
possess a periscope,

tell myself it won't hurt
to reach out, to blink

to touch the ice.

At Dawn, Harp Music is not Your Voice

your voice is gravel,

the way you touch me is sun,
I cling to missing you.

Fine.
I walk for days in the cold and weeds,
clouds and winter fall around me,

melt into mud,
wind permeates space behind
my neck,
under my ears,
around my ankles.

I lower my face,
my eyelids burned
by wind.

Home: your eyes and lips light up,
I gaze upon them,

but it is your fingertips,
that warm the valley
between my shoulders,

my clavicle,
my forearms,
my hip bones,

not shelter,
not blankets,
not lamps.

I use your fingers to map my body
to feel where I've burned life,

who I touch.

Eat Clean

This dessert buffet is all clown noses with queen bee sauce, Andy Warhol's white wigs pop, a dollop of presumption over H and M Pizza grease, an embarrassed slide down the aisle. We want to smother ourselves with sprinkles and pink paper. We want tangerine sky and green hair. Who is eating out Disney? Darling close your eyes, stick out your tongue. Wait for the rush and fall. This ride won't hurt. I'm sorry it's only papier-mâché strawberries. The sweetness: fake. It felt so real for a second. I'll treat you like a Victorian powder wig. Present you, stretch you over some good hard wood that we can eat like bacon. Don't move. Photography hasn't been invented yet. This exposure to something new may take a while.

Aragonite (CaCO₃)

you say a dinosaur protects you at night while you float
        alone through outer space / I'm shivering at
3 am and someone's climbing the stairs / armor deteriorates
        / melting in a mostly iron atmosphere at
the earth's core. / *These clusters are called "sputniks."*/ Would
        you rather sink in solids or liquids? / We
work so hard just to stand in our *pristine expansion,*
then we get stronger / we have a hardness level of 5. /
        Aragonite provides a safe base from which to
explore new possibilities.
What levels will I go just to / find you next to trees / or *an*
        alternate reality / and at what climbing
elevation? / You record your *colored bands in the matrix*
        daily / the internet tells me who I should be
friends with every hour / what degree of closeness they
        resemble.
Self-discipline and centering / both begin, *to steady nerves* /
        place on the solar plexus / *orange calcite feels*
different on the ground / falling from the air yesterday /
        other things on the ground tore my arms up

/ the ground is not always best. / *Carnelian is mistaken for*
      Aragonite / does not have internal fractures
but we kid ourselves / *veils are not linear.*

Note: words in italics taken from *Essential Guide to Crystals* by Simon and Sue Lilly, 2006, 2010, and 2018. published by Watkins Media Limited. United Kingdom.

Doris Day Octapussy

after Jessica Kallista's collage exhibit: "Dear Suburbia" Fairfax,
VA.

Jessica's Hollywood sneer
and tentacle slush invade the bedroom,

each opaque leg a single monster
suction cup probing my gray matter,

the sparrow crashes the window
at the exact moment I hunger

for red lips: not to kiss
but to own—the steadfastness of the jaw,

I want to smother myself in teal shag
carpet but I need to board this UFO first.

Hightail it out of here
on a mermaid's tail sheen.

So buffed and camera ready,
please zipper up my third eye.

See, the pull tab zipper makes it easy.

vacuum

after Jessica Kallista's collage exhibit: *"Dear Suburbia" Fairfax, VA*

The woman likes to push it around:
control it from the top wearing her
tight black panty hose:

push it,
pull it,
heave it up the stairs.

The machine roars in pleasure or protest—it doesn't matter.
Children and small dogs flee this noise,

open wide,
suck up the dirt,
swallow it,
keep it down.

Dust balls, cat hair,
a Lego,

pieces of paper.
It's all appetite.

Don't miss a drop. She likes it
dirty, knowing she cleans up nice.

Sometimes the vacuum hose becomes
unfastened from its secure post,
the dog hair spat back onto the carpet.

She forces the vacuum to lick it up again,
scolds it, pushes it faster this time until

the floor is slick and shiny,
until she's sweaty,
the work finished
on this newspaper Sunday.

She perches a winged back chair,
surveys the living room, shoves
the vacuum back in the closet, tight,
a little rough.
She washes up, goes out, satisfied.

Her Hair is the Bomb

After Sabrina the Teenage Witch Reboot

subtle curl,
toss of snark,

a wrenching suck,
her spells: crosswords,

the aunts in the kitchen gossip about the Church of Night's
new High Priest and bake,

metaphorical pebbles shoved down neighbors' throats
while sleeping,

animate a stolen prom dress
so it dances in the pet cemetery,

fill in missing time spaces in gym lockers
where a skull should be,

the Hecate moon glints off sparks
on rainy day nails.

At report card time
her lips dry up a party mansion,

shred a cheerleader sweater at midnight,
pencil shavings to burn,

it's the wind and the tulips.
She cannot stand

outer world pretty objects waving
through glass, her black cat

meowing and thriving,

her bats and spiders
in the fridge.

She's promised to the
Dark Lord. Signs her name in blood

just to save her friends' lives,

this girl will make your torso so tight
you'll miss your heart.

She grips homework papers like sloth toes,
meets counselor appointments

 wearing cute shawls,

demons from the deep mines
barely lumber into mac n cheese tv dinners,

shield her house with salt,
it's not a chamber for a human boyfriend,

he's too delicate,
sleep changes his affection,

her striking distance an escape for a bit,
these tiny grimoire sighs

her to do list:

torture. check.
smile to the world. check.
solve dead father's puzzle. check.

the biggest mask
she glues to your face.

The Permian Age:

earliest reptiles appear

I don't remember whose idea it was. One
day after school the Maiasaura stomped to

Walmart, leaving her reptile son, and
his Eoraptor friend with me alone in the

Midwest cave. We were supposed to
intuit better, feel the meteor coming.
Let's take turns, scrape our claws

on each other's scales, nails to skin,
down the front of clothes.

Three pairs of hind legs backed
into canned peas, Campbell's soup,

linguini noodles and red, red beets.
Metal lids and Spaghetti O

faces shined and sweated
in the dark, the light bulb string

pulled into oblivion, the sun broken.
The glacier covered the earth slowly

melting with an air conditioner drip —
what I ravaged: everything soft and pretty

swirled through a clock stopped universe
like decorative marbles.

Then: the fire.
Terrible tongues warning prey,

the wood paneled room exploded in burn
and screeching. I ran. The Maiasaura

grabbed me by the torso, her talons
raked my shoulder and clavicle.

Her offspring got it worse. I heard him wailing somewhere
in the dark.

I stared at paper flowers and
black and white dioramas.

The Maiasaura found me hiding.
My face changed in the mirror

as her limb struck me, the arm pulling back
again and again. Pale exposed

scales turned pink, then red.
Inside the prey became predator dreamt

of landing a blow to the head.
Huddling in the fire's fall out,

the flowers burned in salt water,
sealed like shed skin

to the floor.

_____ : set it on fire

Janet's real hair doll
forced tea tree oil beauty regime
dirty sex wish list
box of teenage years journals
tomb stone price list
toaster instructions
2004 map of Arkansas
ex's converse tennis shoes
ex's printed out texts
too small bralette
ten-year-old tax returns
Ziplock bag of baby teeth
thrift store postcard of someone else's family
Aunt Josephine's shitty muffin recipe
old e-mails of ex best friend
floppy disc filed under **evidence**
love ritual candle: pink
anger ritual candle: red
money making ritual candle: blue
witch lost item spell #32 items: Lavender, white candle,
twine, one rock

yoga mantra #2: the universe is a safe place for me to be.
how to be happy manual second edition

Serpentine ($Mg_6(OH)_8Si_4O_{10}$)

She said when did a growler become a thing? You stem a
    snake bite.
What do you go numb with at night? In Serpentine's
    patterning *fibrous is poison,*
but the more massive you are, the more safe.

This is just a format to reveal my feelings while I teleport to
    other peoples' parties,
you are in awe and then you pull a classic cancer of being
    both on land and in the sea simultaneously.

How to penetrate the shell and *allay fears,*
all *mind whirring* on this cliff integrate a new state of
    awareness,
microcrystalline Serpentine.
Develop psychic powers,

come back for me in fog,

put your ear to my crux, / listen above my head

Note: words in italics taken from *Essential Guide to Crystals* by Simon and Sue Lilly, 2006, 2010, and 2018. published by Watkins Media Limited. United Kingdom.

Dubuque, Iowa: Summer

A shutter on a camera blinks so fast / a deer disappears into
  woods
white puffy clouds easy to capture / a June moon: not so
  much
looks like a flashlight under the covers / the bodies in
  between—wear denim cut offs
the chess players at the next table / drinking a flight of beer
dancing in the tiny kitchen camper / dancing by the fire to
  Lord Huron
mosquitos avoid the campfire smoke /a whisper of fall wind
  / flashes over bare shoulders

like changing our mind

Preseli Bluestone (composition varies)

Do I cherish these rare five-thousand-year-old plants like
        your calf muscles?
I haven't seen skin in days / all makeshift auras from a
        Wales
carpenter and rock opera charisma.

Burn a new romance record *in the air,*
it's the little things in the desert doorway *dimensions,*

the sprig of energetic ash colored grass,
the mountain lion half asleep,
connects us with the past,
people write in essay form to extract feeling.

Find the mud route in the dark,
private homebodies of sheltered water.

How to cross that collapsed highway bridge,
the *Neolithic people* step all over it.

Shells on a cliff up high.

How did they get there? We know but don't talk about it.

Note: words in italics taken from *Essential Guide to Crystals* by Simon and Sue Lilly, 2006, 2010, and 2018. published by Watkins Media Limited. United Kingdom.

Pool Parties III: Dessert Buffet

This dessert buffet is an open all night,
clown nose catastrophe

with extra queen bee sauce
and Rachael Ray know how.

Dip my fingers into this sugar bowl.
Pizza is street smart, carries a knife.

We don't want your heavy sauce,
we want tangerine sky
and open-air lawn smothering

green old lady hair
and pink pig dip truffles.

Who is eating who?
The sex advice column doesn't know anymore.

Close your eyes, stick out your tongue,
oh I'm sorry it's papier Mache.

It felt so real for a second.

Zoosk Online Dating for Her

She gleamed in white and red, said I viewed you once, messaged twice. He climbed the keys to create sentences, then paragraph mountains of white snow. Purple square thumbnails, got a text, a retweet, a future sext. She liked his hair in his face like riff raff. She stared, scared that she lost truth last summer. She looked for it in mini-skirts, teal eye liner, Murakami novels. He searched her two-inch boxes: I'm here, alive. Thighs parted within 50 miles. Hair swept up within 25 miles. College educated or not. Pets or not. Chalk up dough. Smile. Close eyes behind mirrors and microwave doors and team banners. Bathing suits. White water rafts. Roman ruins. She looks for her care-free, spinning around in a circle, looking for itself. It is urban planning through Under Armor tee shirts and tuxedos, but she lost the map.

Ranch for Sale. As is.

For Chris.

In the god trees you disappeared into Port wine and too many off ramp brown eye role playing games. My heart in a 1960s ranch style basement. Thought you'd come in, shake out the red and white checkered tablecloth, pull aside the daisy patterned curtains. Thought the room would get a make-over: eggshell finished canary yellow paint and hard wood floors. Instead I'm glued to this bar stool at an orange Formica counter-top where none of the stains lift. I pretend a teenager takes my order. Egg cream please. Owe me real vinyl. Windex the gold painted starburst mirror. The dividing wall hasn't been bulldozed yet, no natural light comes in. Assume a stoic manikin pose complete with immovable jaw lines. A flash of glint, a swirl of curl, a mod con gray slip-on shoe. It's crazy to want someone around after a three-day conversation and a cold fish salad, but I was starving for a glossy musical reprieve, for spell check autonomy, for remodeling this lack of a dehumidifying underground. I assume my ventricles needed a lift, thought you would be the contractor for the job, but casualness creates a fiery death. I'm not that kind of light ribbing panty hose commercial. I'm out of Kleenex and tongue kissing. Are you going to buy the place or not?

_ _ _ _ _ _ _ _ : great work of art

stuffed cow stomach in oils

flesh colored 1890s red head

burnt hambone and eggshell

grimacing priest holding his own neck

lamb face next to a knife

powdered wig on a vestibule

prostitute in garters on a swing

closed mouth geranium

super bug

mansion glowing orange against tornado darkened sky

soldier split open over one pike

sun rays gleaming over tiny church yard

sweating jazz pianist

rotting ham with flies

breast

breast

neck and shoulder

clavicle

old brown boot

dead grandmother

dead husband
dead wife
feet with ants on picnic blanket by the Seine

The Telephone Operator Knows When to Plug in

the operator whispers "quixotic"
illegally enters the conversation

mouths "cabin crew"
and "patient zero" She (I) am made deaf

I haven't seen the sun for days
but I heard it once

a mixture of arrows and static
every word a broken economy

the operator resonates in outer space
presses all of the wrong

buttons and expects a different outcome
each time

it's not the line I was looking for
but the blood in my veins turns stagnant

a bread line moves faster
which pleases the operator

since returning to Russia
in the past, sits behind a scratchy curtain

eyebrows like daggers
a speech class weapon

eyes and lips
call me a Slavic slur

the snow on the line falls
over icy insults

the scrabble dictionary sluggish
give me your dirt

the operator whispers
plays the soundtrack to the

The Third Man
listens in, but this isn't Orson Welles

in black and white beauty
it's our own Vienna getaway

and the operator is taking notes
tired of the spoken word

the codes change too fast:

"A red dress flies at_____"
"opulence colors my_____"

cut-throat with a snap
I hear the busy signal

my voice falters
free fall streaming and radio world

all of the dimes fall from behind my ears
try to crawl toward my eyes

I'm a reborn manikin
the operator breaks the fourth wall

dresses me for the opera
I wear a dial up receiver hat and electrical

tape purse, a bodice covered in numbers
the operator always wanted to say "you look like

a million," injects me with a syringe
retires to a box seat

I. The melting point of dry granite is 2500 degrees Fahrenheit

The angel in the cemetery: put there for protection,
a curved backs slopes and means safe passage,

eight-foot wings smothered by a green patina
overnight: barely moss colored, dank, old.

The white flew away with the doves,
the artist signature barely legible;

legend says the woman learned of a
terrible secret: turned the statue's wings from white to
      black,

her pain folded into layers,
hard feathers fall all around her, mixes with the autumn
      dead,

every tear that falls within these gates, fingers mingle
along the cemetery path the angel grimaces.

II. You tried me on once

The angel hears your name,
hears my murmuring shoulders tremble at dusk,

the sun is setting.

I press: I'm unnamed, un-glossed.
A tremoring clavicle from laughter drenched in other's
            bitterness,

flip to bewilderment at real time photographic images
of dead people who used to be cheek blush and paisley
            shirts.

This one in an all poster ready prep: casual business attire,
the collar, the tie, the loafer.

This wife Evelyn in 80s Rhea Pearlman disguise,
frizzy hair and round glasses,

thought I'd be struck down
by lightening for laughing so hard

in a cemetery. You showed me the stone children
and the frogs in their pockets, the hummingbirds on their
        sleeves,

the loose change—people's wishes and hopes,
left coinage and hightailed it outta there

before death could remind them,
the dead trees against the blue sky growing darker.

The ghost angel follows us,
tries to remember the feel of walking,

wants feeling back in her left hand
(some of her fingers were sliced off by vandals),
couldn't have been a clearer truth.

III. I feel nothing but light,
your voice, the way you put your hands

in your pockets when you talk to a student,
unassuming, the smile on your house

that you can wash off later
in quiet whiskey poured in small rooms

where Argentinian poetry sits on a
table waiting to be translated.

You said you like picking up things
that others gave away— the unloved things.

The way you hold your rock
up to the sun to fight

malevolent forces in the
hallway and unsympathetic mouths

over car phone speakers: they cannot deter you
and this feeling that now I'm the protector,

to bask in your play
and crinkle that is orange.

Your smooth gray slip on shoes that I glance at,
the wishing to invite you to state parks

but not wanting to scare you away
while your heart seals up, forms a salve.

Your lips that smelled like cloves,
hesitant hands, how could I not

grow six feet to protect you
like the black angel?

But she is looking down
and I'm looking up,

I guess that's love,

to harness a shadow from inside
rage against monsters,

to feel our skin grow as strong as rock.

come look at this view

rocks say *egress*
say *buttress*

a water-wall face
form menaces

says *jump dummy*

a girl's Nike toes dipping
a cliff's edge

she likes to play a game
get too close

on a sun and wind pop novel day
smack gum and wink and kiss

the great west

isn't bison and boots

its

teeth too close
the non-secret

parts of bodies

of skeletons
scrambling up slate rock

of tongues dueling for a hot minute
gecko guests look away

daring us to live a little
to cop a feel of rock on ribs

to end the tightness
all the not knowing

the bird beaks in throats

the yearning to feel and not feel

a view or swallowing
a life too far behind

to catch up

Gone Girl

Inspired by Songwriter Gayla Drake's Persephone

Persephone left me— a shadow in rain,
she used to lag behind anyway,

dragging, assaultive weeds grabbing
at her ankles pulling her toward dirt

like they knew
where she'd end up,

she fell on long runs in dandelions,
we felt something watching,

one morning she was gone,
I called my shadow on a broken cell phone,

it had to be broken to reach the underworld,
she said *come visit,*

she'd send a boat for me
in the middle of land at midnight

to carry our future past selves back to one another.
It was a special occasion. I wore a dress

to see if our bodies could stick
like smacked lips,

like flour on sweat,
I wanted her skinny forearms again

to hold my books,
to lean my back and hair into.

I wanted her to solidify

like gum under seats,
but she said she couldn't leave

cause she had an appetite.
What else does he feed you?

I couldn't touch her,
the visit seemed to last a month

though I disappeared for just twenty minutes
staring at her pomegranate mouth,

later I shone a flashlight on my naked
body looking for fingerprints

on my wrist,
looking for signs of transformation,

that time she held my digits tight
racing hot air balloons above us in summer,

fortressing under my quilt
when thunder banged the sky,

it was all wind
warning me,

teasing my eyelid dreams,
making an appearance in the doorway

at 3am. All visions show up then,
or holograms or fictional Greek torsos in fog

or dogs, licking my legs,
wanting a taste of above ground.

I feel her laughter sometimes
in my gut, knowing someone

puts on a show, fluffs her hair, gives her a squeeze,
a shuffle around the watery soul community,

maybe not,
something watches me at night now,

it's not her,

the tiny hairs on the back of my knees

stand up, the candles flicker,

I hear her mother weeping, the air freezes,

I hear the dogs whining, claws scratching

outside my bedroom like they followed her home,

like she somehow escaped.

She's so close for a second
I feel her fear at getting caught,

she wants to get under my blanket,

something's about to shake.

_____ : is a four-legged word

your forehead
airplane angry baby
naked gardener
broken break up ceramics
recycled trash fiction
empty wine bottle
the crane we didn't know what it was
allergic runny eyes
questionable stain on a trench coat
stolen gem ring at the gym
salmonella
dead deer by the side of the road
that dream about that jerk boy
a parent looking through a peep hole
a malfunctioning lawnmower in a movie

Pool Parties IV: Those Antlers Look Hot on Your Baby

Finger a cupcake, lavishly.

Bare a bloody skateboard.
Sock it to the skull breaker.

Jaw chaser, alarm explosion.

Heavy metal,   canal,   candy pop,   Portishead bunny.

Red Hots 2000.

Book starch this shrunken head to bits.

Satellite silver sex tray.
Dot to dot animal voice.
Glint of golden wedding:
she is sexy on repeat.

Play duct tape on a one-handed piano.

Meteorite (composition varies SiO_2 vs. $Fe_2O_3(T) + MgO$)

For Ken

on the back of your motorcycle
thought to be descended from heaven,
I see the moon
actually falling
from the sky
and the smells change
from wildflowers, to factory,
to creek.
My hands grip your waist
so tight I cannot write later,
open new levels in me,
your fingers
a new horizon,
feel busy
but graze my bare knee
checking in,
which is *rare but found anywhere,*
my awareness

is safe like
the remains of a large planet.
I close my mouth to keep bugs out,
breathe through my nose
until back at the camper
I pretend I am not scared
to live.

Kyanite (Al_2SiO_5)

come back for me,
hardness depends on a direction.
I'll be hot turbine and thin and turn in clover,
meet this goat herder walking in *parallel striations,*
she walks where she isn't supposed to, tranquil,
the rainwater *acts as a catalyst,* cuts roads into mud and
quiet,

her feet disappear into days,
makes rapid links between all things.

Note: words in italics taken from *Essential Guide to Crystals* by Simon and Sue Lilly, 2006, 2010, and 2018. Published by Watkins Media Limited. United Kingdom.

Trapped in the Paint Store

A tiger's eye stared me out of gold once.
It said, *give up what you love.*

I dug my way back through beetles, water, and oil.
So many colors to get me wet every day I could not label
emotions under easels.

Am I *Sienna Italy?* Am I *Frosted? Knight time brusque?*
Yellow wasps break in through a crack in the atmosphere,

swarm under tiny, wood bones, heave our auburn hair into
        a cluster:
we shelter in the stock room.

Live nudes dance through the aisles.
Regrow their arms under matte sky blue indoors.

Lovers picnic in rose and melon,
wolves roam looking to grey ghost and party hard.

These beasts do not understand humanity—only exposed
    necks.
A twentieth century shade buries a friend,

green bottle flies bite everyone in the eyes.
Our same bleach nightmare—in tourniquet shadow.

A poison that erases and smears all primary colors, all the
    right answers,
finishes its stain test.

Wake up.

a bare mineral intermission

an evening curtain lifts on the summer solstice / the tree dancer is late / branches reach up /

stash a twig prop under the stage / a step and leave root / the universe takes the dense and most gorgeous / salve these blue birch legs / the forest floor loves me and a thicket of moans / red throated birds sing fire onto cheeks / the end is a painting after all / my flight is moon / a show of waning / fall despair / the romance language of us swaying / it takes $1/5^{th}$ of a glance from you to increase my fortune / build the necessary shelter forts from your forehead / your Orion neck / too above me to hear confessions / to clap confusion into yesterday. / Is nesting his or hers? These are two dramatic questions / all theater nails a mark.

Notes on an Episode of Midnight Gospel

all names have been changed

Trenchia is a warrior in the world of death that she entered by mistake. / She carries a rose in her mouth that absorbs blood / turns into a sword when she needs to fight a beast / her horse looks like a robot horse but breathes air and loyalty / the blond boy follows her around. / Across the city, a demon spins in the body of a man until the man is split in two / sometimes the man is upside down and spins on his head / Trenchia says that *you have to forgive, you have to listen* / the blood absorbs into her and she uses that to fight the demon / she saves her love at the end and they kiss and she is taller than him but then the demon is rebirthed / it covers the world in green slime and hate and murders everything in the city / the world gets swallowed up in green light and everyone is enlightened in their death and in their love / but we miss Trenchia.

Pool Parties V: Photo Op

I walk to the pool party I wasn't invited to; Greta Garbo is there, talking to a script writer that was blacklisted; she is spooning chocolate pudding into his mouth and laughing uproariously; he looks uncomfortable but also like he needs the pudding; this pleases me though it is terribly hot out but no one is in the pool; Joan Crawford is passing a cocktail to Myrna Loy who rolls her eyes under a sunhat while Spencer Tracy hands me a robe; I feel his depression through the terry cloth and they all look at me expectantly like I am the savior of their union, their list maker, their dream planner, their landscaper who lost topiary shears in the wrong neighborhood; now Clark Cable puts a palm on my waist, so we are basically, engaged, but I want to be wooed by these haircuts and teeth; my tap dance starts slow but I build momentum: I wear a bowler hat, grow a cane out from my wrist, I instantly grow a Charlie Chaplin mustache— it's real on me, when I say tap dance I mean my rousing speech and when I say rousing speech I mean I lay down on a lounge chair to take a nap; I've been drugged by glamour: let someone else manage this nuthouse.

Acknowledgments

Some of these poems have been previously published in the following journals:

Prelude, Constellations, Grist, The Meadow, Prometheus Dreaming, Thirteen Myna Birds, Wild Roof Review, Zombie Logic Review, Five:2:One, Vegabond City, Entropy, 8 Poems Journal, Biscuit Root Drive, Waxing and Waning, Disquiet Arts, Goldwake Live, Quiddity, Zone 3, Phantom Drift, Global Poemic, Uppagus, Dream Pop, Drunk Monkeys, Across the Margin, Ethel, The Westchester Review, and Thimble.

"___rooms I would build" was performed in the "Write One/Act One" video pandemic project performed by Bonita Oliver and directed by Alexandra Gray.

The "rock" poems were published in a chapbook called *Teeth Have a Hardness Scale of 5* by Sputnik and Fizzle Press.

The poems "come look at this view" and "The Telephone Operator Knows When to Plug in" were also published in a chapbook *The Female Citizens of Sunshine Nation Face off with Light Sucking Demons* published by Grey Book Press.

About the Author

Jennifer MacBain-Stephens (she/her) went to NYU's Tisch School of the Arts and now lives in Iowa where she is landlocked. Her fifth, full length poetry collection, "Pool Parties" is forthcoming from Unsolicited Press in 2023. She is the author of fifteen chapbooks. Some of her work appears in *The Pinch, South Broadway Ghost Society, Cleaver, Dream Pop, Slant, Yalobusha Review,* and *Grist.* She is a member of the Iowa City Poetry Council and the director of the monthly reading series *Today You are Perfect,* sponsored by the non-profit Iowa City Poetry. Find her online at http://jennifermacbainstephens.com/.

About the Press

Unsolicited Press is based out of Portland, Oregon and focuses on the works of the unsung and underrepresented. As a womxn-owned, all-volunteer small publisher that doesn't worry about profits as much as championing exceptional literature, we have the privilege of partnering with authors skirting the fringes of the lit world. We've worked with emerging and award-winning authors such as Shann Ray, Amy Shimshon-Santo, Brook Bhagat, Kris Amos, and John W. Bateman.

Learn more at unsolicitedpress.com. Find us on twitter and instagram.